Enjoy Being Proud of Who You Are

52 Inspirational Life-skills Messages for Teenagers

Peter Nicholls

Enjoy Being Proud of Who You Are
52 Inspirational Life-skills Messages for Teenagers

Copyright © 2013 Peter Nicholls and Associates Pty Ltd, Adelaide, Australia

Enjoy Being You – How Leisure Can Help You Become the Person You Want to Be at *www.australiaspeoplegardener.com.au*

How to Create Your Second Adulthood – Planning your transition from full time work to 'whatever is next in your life'. at *www.australiaspeoplegardener.com.au*

ISBN: 978-0-9923909-2-1 (ebk)
ISBN: 978-0-9923909-3-8 (sc)

This ebook edition 2013 by DoctorZed Publishing

DoctorZed Publishing books may be ordered through booksellers or by contacting:

DoctorZed Publishing
IDAHO
10 Vista Ave
Skye, South Australia 5072
www.doctorzed.com
61-(0)8 8431-4965

This book is copyright. Apart from fair dealings for the purposes of private study, research, criticism or review, as permitted under the Copyright Act, no part may be reproduced by any process without written permission from the author or publisher.

The author of this book does not dispense medical advice nor prescribe the use of any technique as a form of treatment for physical or mental problems without the advice of a physician, either directly or indirectly. The intent of the author is only to offer information of a general nature to help you in your quest for enjoyable leisure and life satisfaction. In the event that you use any of the information in this book for yourself, which is your right, the author and the publisher assume no responsibility for your actions

Layout design by Anna Dimasi

WHY I WROTE THIS BOOK:

In this 21st century frenetic lifestyle era, teenagers are crying out for help in how to prepare and cope with the impending jungle of adulthood. This is evidenced in the appalling growth – worldwide - in the incidence of teenage depression and suicide. I was amazed and appalled at the precious little I found written specifically for teenagers on life-skills messages of the type contained in this book.

Forty years of working professionally in recreation and sport development has given me extensive insight into

- positive behaviour by people of all ages and backgrounds enjoying their favourite leisure and recreational pursuits
- the passions, talents and unique potential that drive people to achieve great things in their lives.

This, plus having been blessed with the gift of listening, the passion for writing and the wisdom not to judge, have given me a sound basis on which to build my lifestyle mentoring business.

Life-skills are timeless attributes, of value to people of all ages and backgrounds. Now in my 70's, the grandparent in me inspired me to pass something of the flame of my life's marathon to the youth of the world, encapsulated in the title of this book:

"Enjoy Being Proud of Who You Are".

A MESSAGE TO EVERY TEENAGER:

You are at a stage of your growing life where nature is taking you through many physical and emotional life changes. You are starting to see life differently.

You are experiencing the transition from being carefree to one of wondering what you have to offer and where you fit in society as you move toward the seemingly jungle-like world of adulthood.

We've all been there and life has taught us many good messages for you.
This book gives you just a few tips to help you along the way.

FREEDOM REQUIRES BOUNDARIES

It's wonderful to feel the freedom of nature, be it in a park, in the hills, by the beach or in any other favourite natural area. While nature seems to run carefree and wild, it lives by and expresses earth's most stringent rules and boundaries. Those rules and boundaries are what make nature so grand, awesome, powerful, delicate and majestic.

Nature intends a blossoming human life to similarly grow freely and majestically but again within life skills, rules and boundaries. People who go outside the law don't have boundaries to guide them. They eventually envy people who do have boundaries – not because they aren't in trouble but because they have learned what real freedom means. This book will help you establish boundaries that best suit your lifestyle, goals and ambitions. When you live and move within these boundaries, you develop the building blocks upon which you can enjoy unlimited freedom to grow, mature and blossom.

How I see life

The following statement is basic to my work as a lifestyle mentor:

- ***When you lose yourself in an interest you love, you find yourself.***
  You are born with unique natural talents that are yours to discover and use. When you use them with passion, you come alive, you feel good about yourself, increasing your self-esteem, self-confidence, self-belief and sense of self-worth. You feel energised, positive, creative and excited. You are growing and expanding as a person.

You're OK! Be comfortable with the fact that the changes you are experiencing in your outlook on life are normal and healthy. Have no fear about the fact that it can be a very difficult time of life to understand. It's a bit like white water rafting. You navigate the rough areas positively, knowing there are still waters waiting for you at the other end.

Contents

Your Potential	1
Your Mental Health	15
Your Relationships	33
Your Self-expression	51
About the Author:	59

YOUR POTENTIAL

What do people say you're good at? When do you find yourself so wrapped up in what you are doing that the time seems to stand still and everything else is forgotten while you enjoy what you're doing?

What creative talents do you know you have? Does expressing them give you an especially good feeling about yourself?

This section of the book aims to give you some ideas about what you might want to do with your life – at work, at home and at play

Exploring your mind

The mind is today's 24/7 work-space, playspace and home-space. Your mind's potential is unlimited so there is always plenty there for you to discover.

THE VALUE OF UNCERTAINTY

Uncertainty is good. Uncertainty starts the process of questioning, searching and finding answers

Big picture

Pursue interests that are bigger than you. You will get more out of life than you ever thought possible.

THAT UNCOMFORTABLE FEELING

Moving out of your comfort zone is an essential stage of growth. Uncomfortable zones offer stepping stones to new comfort zones and greater success.

Born to blossom

You're like a sapling tree - young and preparing to surge into awesome maturity. Enjoy the process of growing and allowing your natural potential to blossom.

Better than "just do it" is "just did it"

"Just do it" is a wish. "Just did it" is a highly satisfying fact.

Mistakes are OK

It is from mistakes that we learn most about ourselves.

THE BIGGER PICTURE

Growing is about seeing what you couldn't see, thinking what you never thought and understanding what you never knew.

Mission possible

When you explore the unknown you first see the obvious, then moving to the improbable and the seemingly impossible, only to find that the impossible becomes possible, then probable, then obvious.

Believe in yourself

Believe in your unique natural talents, including talents you don't yet know you have. They can take you wherever you want to go in life.

Enjoy being different

You are different to anyone in human history.
Life's best opportunities lay in what makes you different.
Your personal power comes from your uniqueness.

DO WHAT YOU LOVE

Do what you love, love what you do and others will love you.

Passion pays

The only reason people might not like a passionate person is because they wish they had the same sense of passion. They will have disappeared from your life when your passion brings you success.

Your Mental Health

You hear lots about how exercise enables you to stay physically fit and healthy, but what should you do to stay mentally fit and healthy?

What sort of mental exercises could you use to keep your mind fit?

Think about what happens to your mind when you have a negative experience and when you have a positive experience. How do you see each affecting your mental health?

This section aims to help you enjoy frequent positive experiences that keep your mind healthy and build your resilience to cope with negative experiences.

Love the person you are

Loving who you are and being proud of what you do is very different from loving yourself.
Don't worry, others can tell the difference.

Don't beat yourself up

It's just as important not to judge yourself as it is not to judge others. Accept yourself for who you are in the same way as others want you to accept them for who they are.

TRUST YOUR FEELINGS

When making decisions, note carefully your initial gut feeling about what seems right or best. It's very often the right decision for you.

STEP OUTSIDE!

Imagine that you could step outside of yourself and watch yourself in action. You will be amazed how much you can see and learn about yourself.

It's ok to cry

To never cry is like a form of emotional constipation. It's natural to let your emotions flow the way nature intended. But crying all the time only gives you a wet handkerchief.

BE KIND TO YOURSELF

It may often seem that success in life is about giving yourself a hard time. Be kind to yourself. Life is a long-distance event, not a sprint.

YOUR HIDDEN STRENGTHS

A tree's root system is wider and higher than what you see. That's what gives the tree its strength. Most of your strength is invisible to others too. And, like the tree, feeding your hidden strengths ensures the visible you is loved and appreciated..

Move on

Sometimes things go wrong and you just have to wear it. Decide to bite the bullet, put it behind you and move on.

Stay child-like

Being child-like is different to being childish.
Keep the child-like, naturally care-free laughter of childhood alive in you. It will always be important to your success in life and relationships.

The ripple effect

Any experience that makes you feel good about yourself has a ripple effect, flowing through to everything else you do and think. You get a fresh, positive view of everything, including your problems and how you can help other people.

Leisure-your ultimate free choice

No one can choose your leisure interests for you.
Truly enjoyable leisure experiences for you express your unique passions, skills and talents.
Being totally in charge of creating your leisure experiences is a powerful way to start taking charge of your life.

Enjoy being your true self

What better way to express yourself, develop your abilities and find your purpose in life than when you enjoy doing something for no other reason than the fun you get out of it.

Persistence pays well

Success requires the right attitude when things are going right and persistence when things are going wrong.
Persistence is not just endurance.
It's a determination to succeed no matter what.

The best

Being the best isn't about winning. It's about enjoying doing the best you can for yourself and for others who want your help.

You are enough

It doesn't mean you have done enough. It means be comfortable in your own skin. You have all the natural resources you need within you to become the person you want to be.

TAKE PRIDE IN YOURSELF

Others take pride in who you are when you take pride in who you are.

Your Relationship

How do you get on with people – of your age, older, younger? What sort of people do you enjoy being with? Think of any special person in your life and what it is that makes them special to you.

Do you agree that, much as we all like spending some time alone, we are basically social creatures, with needs to belong with "your kind of people"? Are they the sort of people who are going to give you a deep sense of life satisfaction?

Would you like to relate to other people better than you do now? This section aims to help you build on your natural talents and the ways you communicate with other people - both in the ways you relate to them and in the ways they relate to you.

The joy of being thanked

One of the great joys in life is having someone say to you "thank you" for using your talents to help them.

THE STRONG SILENT TYPE

Caring is a silent positive strength. Your actions say more than words about how much you care about someone..

CARING IS A TWO-WAY STREET

If you want people to care about you, you need to do some caring about others too.

Get real

The best friendships are face to face, not facebook to facebook.

CREATING LASTING FRIENDSHIPS

Enjoy making friends with positive, like-minded people. They are the sort of friendship others need from you too.

Make friends with nature

You are part of nature's family so treat nature as part of your family.

Self-esteem doesn't mean others-esteem

Self-esteem is what you think of yourself, not what others think of you. And if you don't like what they are saying, keep smiling - it will annoy the hell out of them.

OTHERS NEED YOUR TALENTS

Your natural-born talents don't have to be the best in the world for others to want and need you to use.

Earn trust and respect

Show respect and trust if you expect to be trusted and respected.

Don't judge

When you judge someone, you are comparing yourself with them. It's not that either of you are right, just that you're different. Keep an open mind and you might learn something from them.

Feeling better

Want to feel better? Do something that makes someone else feel better.

Be thankful

Be grateful for everything in your life – the good things, the hardship, the obstacles and the failures.
They all give you the strength and resilience to cope with most things life throws at you.

Sharing your problems

It's ok to keep your private thoughts to yourself. When a problem becomes more than you can manage, talking about it with a trusted other itself brings emotional release. Often they too have known the same problem.

Walk tall

You walk tall when you have a big success. It's just as important to walk tall when problems make you want to drop your head.

ACHIEVING SUCCESSFUL RELATIONSHIPS

You will be judged not by what you're good at but by your relationships with people.

A Person of Worth

Explore and enjoy your unique self, the hidden self whom the world is waiting to appreciate as a person of worth.

Believe in yourself

You will only get others to believe in you if first you believe in yourself.

Your Self-expression

How do you best express yourself? I don't mean what do you talk about or how you say it. I mean what are the ways you most enjoy expressing your natural talents. For you those talents could be physical (eg sport) or mental (eg music or the arts).

Your talents and passions only have meaning when you express them creatively in ways that are meaningful for you.

This section aims to help you explore ways in which you can enjoy purposefully expressing your true talents, for your own benefit and also to help other people.

BE BOLDLY CREATIVE

Every person is born with creative talents waiting to be developed, be it through music, the arts, drama, or sport, through the mind, body or spirit. It's more about creative expression than creative excellence.

Learn to listen and listen to learn

Listening is the way to learn. When you're talking, you're interrupting your learning.

TEACHING AND LEARNING

*What you're taught often doesn't stick around.
It's what you learn that stays with you for life.*

Keep it simple

Simplicity is a sign of clear thinking. The simplest ideas are often the most practical.
People understand you better when you say things simply.

PEOPLE WANT YOUR ENERGY

Be enthusiastic, energetic, creative and innovative. People are impressed more by the energy and enthusiasm you put into what you do than what it is that you do.

Ready. Fire. Aim.

Don't wait around…just go for it!. Having something in place to improve beats having nothing in place at all.

And one for the parents...

Loving your teenage son or daughter is not enough. He or she needs to feel that you appreciate them as a blossoming human being, whose talents and uniqueness require constant nurturing, support and encouragement, whose dreams are sufficiently intriguing to be worth exploring.

About the Author:

Peter is a Lifestyle Mentor, operating as Australia's People Gardener –Nurturing Human Nature. That title totally befits the person he is - his deep understanding of people, their talents, passions, strengths and desire to blossom to their unique potential.

Peter has learned much about positive human behaviour through more than 30 years of working professionally with people of all ages and backgrounds in the area of parks and recreation development. He is a Recreation Planner by profession, being one of the pioneers of the recreation profession in Australia. He is a past national president and life member of his professional association Parks and Leisure Australia and has received numerous local, national and international awards for outstanding service to his profession.

Peter walks his talk by enjoying a harmonious mix of his passionate interest in lifestyle mentoring with his personal life passions, particularly singing tenor in two choirs, playing weekly golf and taking walks with his partner Carol and dog Oscar. Peter has two children and six grandchildren and lives in Adelaide Australia.

Peter's business website is at
http://www.australiaspeoplegardener.com.au

www.ingramcontent.com/pod-product-compliance
Lightning Source LLC
LaVergne TN
LVHW051511070426
835507LV00022B/3060